STELLA FEEHILY

Stella Feehily is a playwright and screenwriter. *Duck*, Stella's first full-length play, premiered in an Out of Joint and Royal Court co-production at the Theatre Royal, Bury St Edmunds, before playing at the Traverse Theatre, Edinburgh, the Royal Court Theatre and the Peacock Theatre, Dublin. Since then she has written *O go my Man* (Royal Court Theatre); *Catch* (written with four other female playwrights; Royal Court Theatre); *Dreams of Violence* (Soho Theatre); *Bang Bang Bang* (Royal Court Theatre) and *This May Hurt a Bit*, a play about the National Health Service (national tour/St James's Theatre, London).

Other works include *How To Get Ahead In Politics* (Arts Theatre) and adaptations of *Love and a Bottle* for LAMDA's long project, *Coppélia* for Ballet Ireland, and Claudio Tolcachir's *The Omission of the Family Coleman*, which was performed at the Theatre Royal Bath. For Irish National Opera she wrote the libretto for *Close*, a short opera composed by Hannah Peel.

Radio plays include *Sweet Bitter* for Lyric FM, *Julia Roberts' Teeth* for Radio 3 and *All of These Things* for International Arts Partnership.

Television includes developments with BBC3, Blue Ink, Expectation and FilmNation. She is currently developing a film with Picture Locked Pics about surfing set in 1980s Ireland.

Other Titles in this Series

Samuel Bailey
SHOOK
SORRY, YOU'RE NOT A WINNER

Mike Bartlett
THE 47TH
ALBION
BULL
GAME
AN INTERVENTION
KING CHARLES III
MRS DELGADO
SCANDALTOWN
SNOWFLAKE
VASSA *after* Gorky
WILD

Jez Butterworth
THE FERRYMAN
THE HILLS OF CALIFORNIA
JERUSALEM
JEZ BUTTERWORTH PLAYS: ONE
JEZ BUTTERWORTH PLAYS: TWO
MOJO
THE NIGHT HERON
PARLOUR SONG
THE RIVER
THE WINTERLING

Caryl Churchill
BLUE HEART
CHURCHILL PLAYS: THREE
CHURCHILL PLAYS: FOUR
CHURCHILL PLAYS: FIVE
CHURCHILL: SHORTS
CLOUD NINE
DING DONG THE WICKED
A DREAM PLAY *after* Strindberg
DRUNK ENOUGH TO SAY I LOVE YOU?
ESCAPED ALONE
FAR AWAY
GLASS. KILL. BLUEBEARD'S FRIENDS. IMP.
HERE WE GO
HOTEL
ICECREAM
LIGHT SHINING IN BUCKINGHAMSHIRE
LOVE AND INFORMATION
MAD FOREST
A NUMBER
PIGS AND DOGS
SEVEN JEWISH CHILDREN
THE SKRIKER
THIS IS A CHAIR
THYESTES *after* Seneca
TRAPS
WHAT IF IF ONLY

Stella Feehily
BANG BANG BANG
DREAMS OF VIOLENCE
DUCK
O GO MY MAN
THIS MAY HURT A BIT

Rhianna Ilube
SAMUEL TAKES A BREAK… IN MALE DUNGEON NO. 5 AFTER A LONG BUT GENERALLY SUCCESSFUL DAY OF TOURS

Lucy Kirkwood
BEAUTY AND THE BEAST *with* Katie Mitchell
BLOODY WIMMIN
THE CHILDREN
CHIMERICA
HEDDA *after* Ibsen
THE HUMAN BODY
IT FELT EMPTY WHEN THE HEART WENT AT FIRST BUT IT IS ALRIGHT NOW
LUCY KIRKWOOD PLAYS: ONE
MOSQUITOES
NSFW
RAPTURE
TINDERBOX
THE WELKIN

Suzie Miller
PRIMA FACIE

Winsome Pinnock
LEAVE TAKING
ROCKETS AND BLUE LIGHTS
TAKEN
TITUBA

Sophie Swithinbank
BACON
SURRENDER *with* Phoebe Ladenburg

Jack Thorne
2ND MAY 1997
AFTER LIFE
BUNNY
BURYING YOUR BROTHER IN THE PAVEMENT
A CHRISTMAS CAROL *after* Dickens
THE END OF HISTORY…
HOPE
JACK THORNE PLAYS: ONE
JUNKYARD
LET THE RIGHT ONE IN *after* John Ajvide Lindqvist
THE MOTIVE AND THE CUE
MYDIDAE
THE SOLID LIFE OF SUGAR WATER
STACY & FANNY AND FAGGOT
WHEN WINSTON WENT TO WAR WITH THE WIRELESS
WHEN YOU CURE ME
WOYZECK *after* Büchner

debbie tucker green
BORN BAD
DEBBIE TUCKER GREEN PLAYS: ONE
DIRTY BUTTERFLY
EAR FOR EYE
HANG
NUT
A PROFOUNDLY AFFECTIONATE, PASSIONATE DEVOTION TO SOMEONE (– *NOUN*)
RANDOM
STONING MARY
TRADE & GENERATIONS
TRUTH AND RECONCILIATION

Phoebe Waller-Bridge
FLEABAG

Stella Feehily

THE LIGHTEST ELEMENT

NICK HERN BOOKS
London
www.nickhernbooks.co.uk

A Nick Hern Book

The Lightest Element first published as a paperback original in Great Britain in 2024 by Nick Hern Books Limited, The Glasshouse, 49a Goldhawk Road, London W12 8QP

Cover image: Shaun Webb Design, SWD

Designed and typeset by Nick Hern Books, London
Printed in Great Britain by Mimeo Ltd, Huntingdon, Cambridgeshire PE29 6XX

A CIP catalogue record for this book is available from the British Library

ISBN 978 1 83904 375 8

Woodland CARBON
www.woodlandcarbon.co.uk
NICK HERN BOOKS
Printed on Carbon Capture paper

www.nickhernbooks.co.uk/environmental-policy

The Lightest Element was first performed at Hampstead Theatre, London, on 5 September 2024. The cast was as follows:

CECILIA PAYNE-GAPOSCHKIN	Maureen Beattie
NORMAN/PROFESSOR VARNEY	Steffan Cennydd
PROFESSOR FRED WHIPPLE	Simon Chandler
BUDD PHILIPS/ PROFESSOR RICHARDSON/ ENSEMBLE	Hari Kang
SALLY KANE	Annie Kingsnorth
RONA STEWART	Rina Mahoney
PROFESSOR SCHWENGER/ENSEMBLE	Simon Markey
PROFESSOR HENRY NORRIS RUSSELL/ PROFESSOR FRANK CABOT	Julian Wadham
Director	Alice Hamilton
Designer	Sarah Beaton
Lighting Designer	Johanna Town
Sound Designer	Harry Blake
Video Designer	Zakk Hein
Movement Director	Michela Meazza
Casting Director	Gabrielle Dawes CDG

This play was originally commissioned by The Manhattan Theatre Club (Lynne Meadow, Artistic Director; Barry Grove, Executive Producer) with funds provided by the Alfred P. Sloane Foundation.

Acknowledgements

Writing a play involving astronomy and astrophysics sometimes seemed impossible, and I needed some help.

Advisers include friends, family, valued colleagues, and professionals who graciously responded to a random email.

Thank you to Thom Burns, Curator of Astronomical Photographs, Harvard Plate Stacks Collection at the Center for Astrophysics | Harvard & Smithsonian. Thanks to the Harvard Archive and staff.

Thanks to the Royal Astronomical Society: Dr Sue Bowler (Editor of *A&G*), Philip Diamond (Executive Director), and Sian Prosser (Librarian and Archivist).

Thanks to *The Harvard Crimson*: Vivienne Germain and Sage Lattman showed me around and talked me through the history of the *Crimson*.

Thank you to Meg Weston-Smith and Dame Jocelyn Bell Burnell for taking the time to speak with me.

Thank you to Julia Smeliansky from the American Academy of Dramatic Arts for arranging my interviews at the Harvard Observatory.

Thank you to Chris Campbell and Jack Doulin for providing me with valuable feedback.

Special thanks to Professor Cecilia Gaposchkin, Chair of the Department of History at Dartmouth College, who allowed me to use some of her grandmother's most famous lines.

Thank you to Greg Ripley-Duggan, who programmed the play and introduced me to Alice Hamilton. Alice was so encouraging and made great suggestions. Also thanks so much to the wonderful team at Hampstead and casting director, Gabrielle Dawes.

Love and thanks to the gorgeous cast and crew of *The Lightest Element*. I was amazed to discover that Maureen Beattie (CPG) was born in Bundoran, County Donegal – the very town in Donegal I grew up in. It was meant to be.

Thank you to Mel Kenyon for never giving up on Cecilia. Mel organised a crucial earlier reading, so thanks to: Zephy Losey, Harriet Walter, Guy Paul, David Rintoul, Archie Redford, Thea Mayeux and Iona Champain.

Thanks to NHB editor, Sarah Liisa Wilkinson, Deborah Halsey, Nick Hern and the team at NHB.

Thanks to Max Stafford-Clark who read endless drafts, gave invaluable advice for improvements and supplied abiding support. Thanks to Kitty Stafford-Clark for her warmth and encouragement.

Finally thanks so much to my long-suffering researcher; astrophysicist and actor, Victoria Porter. She guided me patiently through the kindergarten stage of astrophysics without rolling her eyes – too much.

S.F.

'I ofen looked up at the sky an' assed meself the question – what is the stars, what is the stars?'

Captain Boyle, Juno and the Paycock, *Seán O'Casey*

'Life can only be understood by looking backward; but it must be lived looking forward.'

Søren Kierkegaard

For my mother

Characters

PROFESSOR CECILIA PAYNE-GAPOSCHKIN, *British, playing twenty-five, fifty-six, seventy-six. Professor of Astronomy, Harvard*

RONA STEWART, *American, playing thirty, fifty. Harvard research assistant and assistant to Cecilia Payne-Gaposchkin*

SALLY KANE, *American, twenties. A student at Radcliffe*

HENRY NORRIS RUSSELL*, *American, fifties. Director of the Princeton University Observatory*

NORMAN MATTISSON*, *American, twenties. A student at Harvard and an 'Editor' at* The Harvard Crimson

PROFESSOR FRED WHIPPLE, *American, Chairman of Astronomy, Harvard, and Director of the Smithsonian Observatory*

BUDD PHILIPS, *a reporter for* The New York Times

MEMBERS OF THE ASTRONOMY DEPARTMENT

PROFESSOR FRANK CABOT*

PROFESSOR DAVID RICHARDSON

PROFESSOR GERHARD SCHWENGER

PROFESSOR JAMES VARNEY*

(* Doubling)

Note on Text

A forward slash (/) indicates when the following line is spoken.

Time Frame

The action takes place in 1925 and 1956, with the opening and closing scenes set in 1977.

Note on Play

Cecilia Payne-Gaposchkin (1900–1979) was a pioneer in astronomy and one of the most eminent astronomers of the twentieth century. She was the first to apply atomic physics to the study of the temperature and density of stellar bodies, and to conclude that hydrogen and helium – the two lightest elements – were also the two most common elements in the universe.

This text went to press before the end of rehearsals and so may differ slightly from the play as performed.

Scene One

17th January 1977. Two hours before an awards ceremony. A stage. American Astronomical Society.

CECILIA PAYNE-GAPOSCHKIN *walks onstage and surveys the auditorium. She has a manuscript in one hand and an unlit cigarette in another.*

CECILIA. Will there be more light than this?

RONA STEWART (*assistant to* CECILIA) *dressed in 1970s style, follows from the wings.*

RONA. We're early. I understand these are 'working lights'.

CECILIA *takes off her coat – revealing a suit that has a timeless quality.*

CECILIA (*muttering as she looks around*). Shouldn't one be able to work in 'working lights'?

RONA. Is that what you're wearing?

CECILIA. What's wrong with it?

RONA. Do you want the truth or an argument?

Beat.

CECILIA. An argument?

RONA (*scolds*). Why didn't you buy something new like I told you?!

CECILIA (*defies*). I like this.

RONA. So did I – thirty years ago.

CECILIA *hands the coat to* RONA.

CECILIA. Is there an itinerary?

RONA (*checking a list*). Soundcheck at five p.m. Welcome drinks in the lobby at six p.m. The guests will take their seats just before seven.

CECILIA. Just before seven, I take a Valium.

RONA (*handing her a little pill box*). You take *half* a Valium. We don't want you asleep. Margaret Burbidge will make her address at seven-fifteen – she will invite you to the podium – which I imagine will be – (*Pointing centre stage.*) somewhere here. Mrs Burbidge will hand you the illuminated scroll. Applause. You knock their socks off with your lecture. Applause, applause.

CECILIA. Thank you for the vivid picture, Rona.

(*Trying to find light.*) Oh for goodness' sake! I can't see a thing.

RONA. The technical staff will be here shortly. Try further downstage perhaps?

CECILIA – *sticking the unlit cigarette in her teeth and trying to read in the half-light – begins her speech.*

CECILIA (*loudly*). 'The reward of the young scientist is the emotional thrill of being the first person in the world to understand something. Nothing can compare with that experience.'

RONA. You don't have to kill yourself. There will be a microphone.

More light comes on the stage.

CECILIA (*calls out*). Thank you!

RONA *pulls out an ashtray from her bag and hands it to* CECILIA.

Thank you.

A projection or a board becomes visible with a picture of Henry Norris Russell alongside the words: 'Henry Norris Russell Prize Lecture. The American Astronomical Society – Cecilia Payne-Gaposchkin. 50 years of Novae'.

RONA. Well, Mrs G – it's there in black and white. The Henry Norris Russell Prize. A lifetime-achievement award. What say you to that?!

CECILIA. I say God or the American Astronomical Society has a sense of humour. And I've been dreaming of him recently. I am as I am now and he is as he was.

RONA. Interesting.

CECILIA. And I still don't like him.

RONA. I have recurring dreams about playing field hockey at Bryn Mawr and am in a constant state of anxiety in case anyone notices that I am nearly fifty.

CECILIA. And do they?

RONA. No! No one even bats an eyelid at this sweating middle-aged woman running with teenagers. Probably some message in that.

CECILIA. When I first met Russell he had mislaid his gloves on the New Haven train. I lent him a pair belonging to my father.

History does not record if he found his gloves but he never returned mine.

RONA. Ain't that just like a man?! Do you want a cup of tea or something stronger?

CECILIA. I want a few moments to gather my thoughts. Maybe a tea. If you don't mind?

RONA. Not at all. I left Serena in the lobby. She is thrilled to be invited to such a grown-up event. She's talking about becoming a scientist…

RONA *starts to leave the stage.*

You'll be an inspiration to her.

CECILIA (*lighting her cigarette*). I hope I'll be an inspiration to me.

CECILIA *finds the spot from which she will deliver her lecture.* CECILIA *looks back at her notes.*

(*With the cigarette between her teeth.*) 'The reward of the older scientist is the sense of having seen a vague sketch grow into a masterly landscape.'

From the lighting box:

TECHNICIAN. Professor Gaposchkin?

CECILIA. Yes?

TECHNICIAN. Just stay there, Professor Gaposchkin. Going dark for a few seconds. Lighting check in five.

She closes her eyes. Darkness and the night sky. The stars appear to pulse in the heavens.

Scene Two

January 1925. The Harvard College Observatory. Cambridge, Massachusetts. A classroom.

It's cold outside and not so warm inside either.

Numbers, words and equations on a large blackboard. Director of the Princeton University Observatory, PROFESSOR HENRY NORRIS RUSSELL, *fifties, shrewd and charismatic, dressed in a suit and high-neck shirt of an earlier era, is looking at the work with some interest – disbelief even.*

CECILIA *has a tray of tea things.*

RUSSELL *backs away from the board; his expression is inscrutable.*

CECILIA. Professor Russell, I'm sorry to have taken so long. The yard is treacherously icy and, there's not much light this late.

RUSSELL. No matter, Miss Payne. It gave me another chance to peruse the current draft of your thesis. In the main, it is a beautiful piece of work. Professor Shapley is keen to have it published.

CECILIA *places the tray on a desk.*

CECILIA. Thank you. I understand that you have noted a problem in the chapter on 'The Relative Abundance of the Elements'.

RUSSELL (*gesturing towards the board*). Yes, a problem indeed. Thank you for setting out your calculations. I understand you've spent long hours studying Harvard's glass-plate collection.

She stops setting out the tea things and comes to the board.

CECILIA. Oh, yes. I studied hundreds of glass plates. Hundreds.

RUSSELL (*indicating the board*). Miss Payne, this theory asserts that hydrogen is powering the starry universe. This is your conclusion – that stars are composed of mainly hydrogen and helium. You don't believe this is real?

CECILIA. Yes. Hydrogen and helium atoms appear to vastly outnumber metal atoms in the atmospheres of stars. Have you seen the figures?

RUSSELL. Atomic theory is a developing science, Miss Payne. I find it poses more questions than it answers. Your handwriting is appalling. Is that an A or a two?

He takes a biscuit from the tray and bites while gesturing toward some blurred numbers.

CECILIA (*alarmed*). Gosh. Sorry. That should be N equals two.

CECILIA *corrects some numbers on the board.*

Is that better?

RUSSELL. No.

(*Pointing to sets of equations on the board.*) How do you explain this?

CECILIA *rewrites another smudged number.*

CECILIA. Oh? Of course. Hydrogen lines reach maximum intensity in the A-type stars –

RUSSELL. Right. Thank you for explaining the illegible. Before we continue, may I ask – are the radiators turned off for a reason?

CECILIA. Ah, they only come on when it's freezing.

RUSSELL. Good God. It is 'freezing'.

RUSSELL *rubs his hands together vigorously.*

I left my gloves on the New Haven train.

CECILIA (*offering her gloves*). Take mine.

RUSSELL. I couldn't possibly.

CECILIA. Please. They were my father's. Perfect for Massachusetts weather.

RUSSELL *pulls on the warm gloves.*

RUSSELL. Aren't you cold?

CECILIA. I became accustomed to feeling like a damp cabbage at Cambridge, and now I rarely notice the cold.

RUSSELL. That great English university is built on reclaimed marshland, of course – the Fens. Yes, yes, I remember entirely the rigours of that climate. How are you finding your new Cambridge, Miss Payne?

CECILIA. Uh, it's marvellous, Professor Russell… I have so much freedom here.

RUSSELL. But I'm sure you must miss your native land.

CECILIA. I miss springtime in Buckinghamshire. I have deep roots there. Payne landowners have been at the foot of the Buckinghamshire Chilterns for centuries.

But RUSSELL *has returned to the board.*

There is no spring in Massachusetts; it's either winter or summer…

RUSSELL. Cambridge University provided no possibility for your postgraduate studies.

CECILIA. Well, indeed. It is a privilege to study at such a forward-thinking institution as Harvard.

RUSSELL (*sympathetic*). It would not be easy to return to a country that does not welcome the academic excellence of women.

CECILIA. I believe it would be the death of me.

RUSSELL. Yes. Astronomy is a calling, and you have answered its call.

He turns away from the board towards the tea things – a gesture that disappoints CECILIA.

Am I to serve myself?

CECILIA *hurries to attend to* RUSSELL.

CECILIA. Allow me. Milk?

RUSSELL. Thank you – a little sugar. You were taught physics by Rutherford and Eddington, I understand.

CECILIA. And Arthur Milne.

RUSSELL. And you were taught the atomic model by Niels Bohr also?

CECILIA. I attended Niels Bohr's epoch-making lectures when he visited Cambridge. Alas, his accent was impenetrable. I learned more from reading his work.

RUSSELL. Poor Niels suffers from a speech impediment. The joke goes that Bohr is just as incomprehensible in his native Danish as he is in English.

CECILIA *nods and smiles. The atmosphere has lightened. She prepares his tea. She awaits his verdict. He sips at his tea, then picks up her thesis and holds it aloft.*

But we digress. Twice now, I have read the current draft. On my second reading, I became convinced that the chapter on Saha's theory of thermal ionisation would be an important contribution to astronomy.

He puts the manuscript down.

CECILIA. Thank you, Professor Russell. Everything fell into place using Saha's theory and I confirmed that the absorption lines indicated different amounts of ionisation at different temperatures rather than variations in element abundances.

RUSSELL. However, the hydrogen conclusions undermine your impressive work. I have been grappling with the hydrogen problem for years, but it is impossible that it should be a million times more abundant than metals in the stars.

CECILIA. Impossible, but the results are impossible to ignore.

RUSSELL. I have gone to the verge of my field in this study and am confident that the composition of the stars is practically identical to that of the Earth. And I am not alone.

CECILIA. Oh, I'm not in complete disagreement on the chemical composition of the stars. It's simply I have found this overwhelmingly high abundance of hydrogen and helium.

RUSSELL (*sharp*). In the stars or on the stars?

CECILIA. In. In the stars.

RUSSELL *turns to the board.*

RUSSELL (*irritated*). These figures must be wrong. This theory then suggests that stars are giant globes constituted mainly of hydrogen and helium gas? No, no, my dear Miss Payne, regretfully I would be unable to approve your thesis in this version. But, please be assured you do have time to revise.

CECILIA. Revise? I've been working on this day and night –

RUSSELL (*referring to the board*). Miss Payne, if the stars are made almost entirely of hydrogen, how is it that the solid bodies of the universe are composed mainly of iron? Where is the missing iron in your figures?

CECILIA. Yes, that's the fascinating thing, you see – it is barely there in –

RUSSELL. Miss Payne, why would hydrogen make up nearly the entirety of the Sun when it is practically absent in the air? The Earth's core is predominantly iron. The meteorites that fall from space are made of iron. The solar spectrum contains an overwhelming number of iron lines. This attests to the uniformity of nature, with iron as its chief element.

CECILIA. But if you could examine the behaviour of the Balmer lines –

RUSSELL. I have. Your theory is as yet a tissue of approximations. And you will be thought simply mad or arrogant if you pursue a theory that rejects the findings of the great scientific minds. Miss Payne, people believe our work is benign and noble, but it is a ruthless business.

CECILIA *nods*.

CECILIA. I'm often called a pushy English girl. I am used to being thought eccentric – therefore –

RUSSELL. Stop there. You are twenty-five. You will be the first person to receive a PhD in Astronomy from Harvard University. Your work will be exposed to intense scrutiny once published by the observatory.

CECILIA. I think I could withstand the scrutiny.

RUSSELL (*patiently*). You don't know what you're talking about.

CECILIA. No. I see it. It's so clear. Isaac Newton said. 'If I have seen further, it is by standing on the shoulders of giants.' I would borrow his phrase except to say that the giants face the wrong direction.

RUSSELL *laughs*.

RUSSELL. No one has ever before accused me of lacking 'vision'.

CECILIA. It's about ways of seeing, Professor. If I may remind you, in the days of Galileo, the Church became too upset even to consider the possibility that the Earth moves around the Sun.

RUSSELL. So you think I am wrong? Do you think Eddington is wrong? We are all mistaken in understanding what stars and the universe are made of? Do you think Einstein is wrong?

CECILIA. On balance, yes. I wouldn't use the word – wrong –

RUSSELL (*bemused but sharp*). Don't you know when to be quiet?

CECILIA. I do understand. There is a sense of order and continuity in the way we see the world and to challenge that is a shock.

RUSSELL. Why are you still talking? You are impertinent. For your own good shut up and learn, Miss Payne. Learn, or you will be finished in astronomy before you even start.

CECILIA. I see.

RUSSELL. Professor Shapley is taking me to South Station in search of my gloves. Could you please let him know I am ready?

The meeting is swiftly drawing to a close, and CECILIA *begins to panic.*

CECILIA. You're going? You've only just got here.

RUSSELL *gives* CECILIA *back her thesis.*

RUSSELL. Look, I'm sorry to be the bearer of disappointing news. I cannot approve this for publication in its current form. It's a great pity.

CECILIA. Yes, yes. You've been very clear.

RUSSELL (*bowing slightly*). Miss Payne.

CECILIA. I will resubmit with amendments.

RUSSELL. Will you? Good. Good. I'm relieved to hear it and look forward to reading the next draft. If you need access to my archive at Princeton, I would be happy to facilitate you in any way. Before presenting your final calculations perhaps you should study my 1914 paper on the composition of the Earth's crust and the solar atmospheres. I think it may be of help.

CECILIA. Thank you. You are very kind. I will let Professor Shapley know you are ready.

RUSSELL. And thank you for the tea and the stimulating conversation.

A mortified CECILIA *leaves.* RUSSELL *is left looking at her numbers. He starts to wipe them away. But he is troubled and has the horrible feeling that* CECILIA *might be on to something. But for now, it's too threatening. He throws the duster at the board.*

No! Impossible.

Scene Three

September 1956. A lively Cambridge restaurant.

Jazz music. Radcliffe student SALLY KANE, *twenty-one. She is the picture of 1950s style with a ribbon in her hair. She is finishing a dessert.*

NORMAN MATTISSON, *twenty (a Harvard undergraduate), is squeaky-clean, good-looking, and wearing a sharp 'day suit'. They look like they belong together. He is writing in a notebook. He looks up just as* SALLY *is scraping her bowl.*

NORMAN (*pushing his dish towards her*). Have mine.

SALLY. I really shouldn't.

NORMAN. Why not? Besides, I like watching you eat.

SALLY (*eating a mouthful*). You like watching everything I do.

NORMAN. This is true.

SALLY. I thought you had news.

NORMAN (*checking over his shoulder before continuing*). Oh, I have.

I was waiting for that table to leave.

John Turner has just been kicked out of Harvard. Caught with a girl in his room.

SALLY. What? You're kidding? A Radcliffe girl?

NORMAN (*confidentially*). A Physics sophomore. It's all been kept hush-hush cos her daddy is one of the big donors around here.

SALLY. We'd better be more careful.

NORMAN. You're telling me. But there's an upside to John Turner's disgrace.

SALLY. Oh yeah?

NORMAN. He was supposed to interview Professor Gaposchkin – an astronomer – for *The Harvard Crimson*.

SALLY. It was on the radio. She's just been made the first woman professor at Harvard. She's famous –

NORMAN. And you have been asking me to put a word in –

SALLY. Did you suggest me? Tell me you did! I've done the comp and keep sending you guys ideas, but no one gets back to me.

NORMAN. The thing about bastions of masculinity is that they tend not to have women around. But –

SALLY. But –

NORMAN. I persuaded the rest of the editorial board that a woman should interview a woman scientist.

SALLY. You did? You really did?

NORMAN. I said you had a science background. Am I right?

SALLY. Not like your buddy John, but I studied Physics at Riverdale – I was a member of the astronomy club. I won't feel intimidated, and you know, I can do whatever research.

NORMAN. You don't have to convince me. I know you can. What do I get in return?

SALLY. My gratitude.

NORMAN. I was hoping for something more specific.

SALLY. I bet you were.

(*Wry.*) You have my undying gratitude. Particularly if it proves to Mom that journalism is a career for girls.

NORMAN. Good luck with that one but it's true, Gaposchkin is a 'woman of the moment' and the more vivid *Crimson* profiles get picked up by the Associated Press.

SALLY. Oh, sweetheart. Thank you.

NORMAN (*refocuses*). Now, have you ever read any of the faculty profiles?

SALLY. Yeah. The articles are pithy – a bit provocative. So is Professor Gaposchkin controversial?

NORMAN *pushes a newspaper across the table to* SALLY.

NORMAN. There's a bit in the *Evening Star* about her. But read on.

SALLY (*scanning the article*). Gaposchkin's husband, a Russian obviously, had a little trouble with the House Committee on Un-American Activities. Uh-huh. I see where you're going. Do you think she's a pinko?

NORMAN. That's what I want you to find out.

SALLY. But – it's a profile – right? It's not the *Crimson*'s agenda to ascertain Gaposchkin's politics?

NORMAN. Yeah but don't just write a puff piece. Make your mark. Besides, it could be extremely useful.

SALLY. Useful for whom?

NORMAN. Okay, so here it is. Not content with being the first woman to be made professor at Harvard – Gaposchkin is now angling to become Chairman of Astronomy. Chairman. How nuts is that?!

SALLY. So you don't like that?

NORMAN. It's a ludicrous prospect.

SALLY. That's harsh.

NORMAN. Come on, Sally. There's a limited number of people who can lead wisely! And this would be a lame attempt by Harvard to appear progressive. It's rattling a bunch of decent folks.

SALLY. Are they rattled because they think Gaposchkin is a communist, or is it because she's a woman?

NORMAN. Sally! The lecture halls of Harvard set the political agenda for a generation. Is Gaposchkin imposing her views on the students?

SALLY. The history department is jammed with liberals but they stick to the syllabus.

NORMAN. Well, let's see if *she* does.

(*Hurt.*) I didn't risk my life fighting commies in Korea to come to a university swarming with pinkos.

SALLY. Sure – I do understand… So you want a precis of her achievements and a bit of her personality. A couple of snarky quotes? Is that allowed?

NORMAN. You can ask provocative questions and get away with it because you're a student and a girl. She won't be expecting it.

SALLY. Okay. But I'm in. I'm really in?

NORMAN (*kisses her hand*). Sally Kane, you're in. Are you happy?

SALLY. Uhh – yes.

NORMAN. Right then, are you ready? Let's seize the moment.

SALLY. Now? I'm meant to be seeing my mom –

NORMAN. No. You've got a Thursday deadline. You need to make an appointment with Gaposchkin.

(*Handing her his notebook.*) I've made a list of questions.

SALLY. Where are we going?

NORMAN. I'm driving you to the Harvard Observatory. We'll talk in the car.

NORMAN *takes* SALLY *by the arm and ushers her out.*

SALLY. But, Norman, my parents… I'm catching a train to Providence in an hour.

NORMAN. Forget Providence. You've got an interview to land.

Scene Four

Harvard Observatory Lecture Hall.

RONA *is standing in front of one of several music stands. She is rehearsing the first movement of Mozart's Symphony No. 41 on a violin. A bassoon can be heard. A trumpet.* RONA *stops and starts sections as they turn pages. She spots* SALLY –

RONA. Yes? Are you the new flute?

SALLY. Oh me? No. Not musical at all. I was told Professor Gaposchkin would be here.

RONA. A lunch break for Mrs G is an opportunity to tackle Mozart's Forty-First – the 'Jupiter' symphony. The professor will be conducting the observatory orchestra for at least the next forty minutes. Is there some emergency?

SALLY. No, no. I can wait.

RONA. I am Mrs Gaposchkin's assistant, Rona Stewart. If you want to book a tutorial, could you be a doll and find me later?

The trumpet blasts a series of notes.

SALLY. No. I'm not one of the professor's students.

RONA (*turning behind her and shouting*). Trumpet! Easy!

SALLY. My name is Sally Kane, and I've been asked to write a profile on Professor Gaposchkin for the *Crimson* –

RONA. Sure, sure. That interview has been cancelled –

SALLY. Yes – Mr Turner is no longer –

RONA. Available? –

SALLY. At Harvard. Yeah, it'll be a nice piece in celebration of her. Any chance of a meeting today, Mrs Stewart?

RONA. It's Miss. You are out of luck. Professor Gaposchkin will be in tutorials all afternoon. She's probably stuck in one now.

The oboe and horn play gently under the dialogue. RONA *joins in playing the violin quite gently.*

SALLY. My deadline is Thursday.

RONA. We all have deadlines.

(*Whispers.*) Is it just me, or does that oboe sound flat?

SALLY. It's my first interview for the *Crimson*. I had to fight for it.

The flat oboe continues to irritate RONA.

RONA. Oh no. That won't do at all.

RONA *turns to move.*

SALLY. Miss Stewart, can't you give me a break?

RONA (*eyeing* SALLY*'s hairband*). No girl over seven should wear a ribbon.

SALLY. I didn't know it was a rule. If you could just give me an hour with her –

RONA *puts down her violin and leads* SALLY *away from the music stands.*

RONA. I can't concentrate with the sound of your anxiety.

Come and find me this evening. I'll see if I can get you an appointment – no promises, mind.

SALLY. Thank you so much.

RONA. Hey, can I give you a tip?

SALLY. Yes, please.

RONA. Don't ask dumb questions.

SALLY. Such as…

RONA. How do you look after your husband, home and three children with a full-time job? She'll switch off.

SALLY. What will switch her on?

RONA. Are you aware that Professor Gaposchkin was the first to discover what stars are made of?

SALLY. I did not know that.

RONA. Tshh! She was the first to discover the origins of matter, the building blocks of the universe, the source of all heat and light, and she knew before anyone else. Her discoveries ripple through time – they pull and stretch every idea that comes after. Without hydrogen – there is darkness.

SALLY. Wow! You're a fan.

RONA. These are simply the facts. Go to the observatory library and acquaint yourself with Mrs G's monograph, *Stellar Atmospheres*. It's fascinating!

SALLY. Sure, ah – to avoid 'dumb questions', may I check something?

RONA. If you're quick.

SALLY *takes out her notebook and pen.*

SALLY. Sergei Gaposchkin is a Russian astronomer here at Harvard. Right?

RONA. Well, he ain't Irish.

SALLY. It's not that I don't admire your terseness, but is there anything else you can tell me?

RONA (*speedily*). Sergei was in exile in Germany just as Hitler was coming to power, and Mrs G met him while on a trip to the Astronomisches Gesellschaft. It was love at first sight. She saved him from the Nazis by getting him a job at Harvard. Is that what you're looking for?

SALLY *writes in her notebook.*

SALLY. You're a doll.

RONA. She knits, plays violin and piano, and writes poetry quite well. Mrs G speaks nine languages, including Ancient Greek and Latin and prefers Lysol to any fancy cleaning brand. Can I go now? I've got Mozart to tackle.

CECILIA, *fifty-six, sweeps in.*

CECILIA. Come along, Rona. Is this the new flute?

SALLY. I'm not musical.

CECILIA *moves towards a music stand with a score.*

RONA. Five o'clock, Miss Kane. Fourth floor. And next time – use the telephone. I'm not a walking diary!

Mozart's Symphony No. 41 – 'Jupiter'. CECILIA *prepares to conduct.*

Scene Five

Harvard Observatory Lecture Hall.

After the Symphony… CECILIA *meets with* PROFESSOR FRED WHIPPLE, *current (1956) Chairman of Astronomy – [her boss] at Harvard, and director of the Smithsonian Observatory. In the background,* RONA *puts away the music stands and sheets.*

CECILIA. Professor Whipple! You took the time to listen. I'm honoured.

WHIPPLE. Is there no end to your talents?

CECILIA. Gustav Holst taught me. Perhaps I've mentioned that before.

WHIPPLE. He had high hopes for you.

CECILIA. Conducting is the only career a man has ever urged me to pursue. Read into that what you will. Well, Fred, it's a novelty to see you.

WHIPPLE. Double-jobbing is killing me.

CECILIA. Your secretary tells me you haven't left the Smithsonian for three days running.

WHIPPLE (*speedily*). Sleep is a waste of time. There's so much to set up. I'll need your help in coordinating how Harvard and the Smithsonian Observatory can combine talents on solar atmospheres and / of course, radio astronomy –

CECILIA. Easy tiger. I think you're a tad over-caffeinated.

WHIPPLE. Pep-U-Up pills. Does what it says on the tin.

CECILIA. Mm-hmm. Wouldn't life be easier if you stepped down from Harvard? You cannot be Chairman of the Astronomy Department and run the Smithsonian effectively. And it's greedy.

WHIPPLE. I'm longing to hand over to you. Believe me.

CECILIA. Do we have a timeline for succession?

WHIPPLE *hands* CECILIA *a copy of the* Evening Star.

WHIPPLE. I wonder did you see this yesterday?

CECILIA. I almost never read the Washington papers.

WHIPPLE *notes that* RONA *is still in the room. He taps* CECILIA*'s arm –*

Rona, could you bring my things up?

RONA. Certainly, Mrs G. Good afternoon, Professor Whipple.

WHIPPLE. Superb playing, Miss Stewart.

RONA. Thank you.

RONA *nods, smiles and leaves.*

WHIPPLE. It's a hint of negative spin about your Harvard tenure.

CECILIA. Well, hit me with it.

WHIPPLE. It teases about the investigation by the House Un-American Activities Committee into Sergei's alleged communist activities.

CECILIA *glances at the newspaper.*

CECILIA. Sergei was questioned a couple of years ago – yes. He was cleared.

WHIPPLE. But you kept it quiet.

CECILIA. Didn't everybody? I had hoped this kind of thing was over.

WHIPPLE. Was Sergei really on a list of Red-ucators in the forties?

CECILIA. Yes, along with every Russian educator in America. Well, I can only say it must have been a slow day in the newsroom.

WHIPPLE. It's just the timing is most unfortunate.

CECILIA. I think you'll find, Fred, that the timing is very deliberate. Why is an old story about Sergei appearing alongside an announcement of my Harvard professorship if not to cause trouble? This lingering McCarthyism is the worst – using gossip to fling around damaging accusations.

WHIPPLE. No one is accusing you, Cecilia.

CECILIA. Okay, but it's the insinuation that is damaging. It makes people wonder if we were communist sympathisers.

CECILIA *suddenly stops. She's near tears.* WHIPPLE *touches* CECILIA*'s shoulder.* CECILIA *gathers herself.*

Endless. It's endless.

WHIPPLE. You could write to the editor.

CECILIA. I could, though I'm not sure I should draw attention to it. This is the problem with conspiracy theories – they cannot be refuted or argued with. They simply remain.

WHIPPLE. Perhaps you're right.

CECILIA. I'll hold my fire until Harvard announces I've been made Chairman of Astronomy. God knows what they'll write then.

WHIPPLE. Pusey and Menzel have asked me to convene a meeting of the Observatory Council to discuss the appointment. The question is – should I delay?

CECILIA (*angered*). Please, no. Don't delay any further. You said you would step down in September.

WHIPPLE. Yes, Cecilia, but the appointment does need a bit of handling. You must agree.

CECILIA. I should have been made Chair years ago.

WHIPPLE. You should have. Everything is a fight, Cecilia. I've had to fight too.

CECILIA. Okay, okay! Should I come to the meeting?

(*Irritated.*) Since I happen to be on the Council.

WHIPPLE (*irritated*). No. You can't be in the room if it comes to a vote.

CECILIA (*irritated*). Are you looking for an excuse to back out? I wouldn't put it past any of you.

WHIPPLE. You're exhibiting a persecution complex, Cecilia. You have many supporters at Harvard. I don't want you at the meeting, but it might be an idea to get some good publicity. Do the old Harlow Shapley trick and trumpet your successes.

CECILIA. Is there any possibility that I will be passed over once more?

WHIPPLE. This is what I am trying to avoid.

President Pusey and the Board of Overseers will take the final decision, of course – but first, we get the department on side.

CECILIA. I've never chased status. The work has always been my passion. But without status, there is no forward momentum.

(*Gesturing to the newspaper.*) We should ignore it for the trash it is.

WHIPPLE *makes a little salute before leaving.*

WHIPPLE. Copy that.

WHIPPLE *leaves. This has just become a bad day for CPG.*

Scene Six

The Harvard Observatory. Astronomy Department. Office of Cecilia Payne-Gaposchkin.

Some hours later. 4.55 p.m. A small cluttered office. The table is a mess of books and papers. Cigarette ash is everywhere. CECILIA *is working through sheaves of papers and smoking a cigarette – the ash has become ridiculously long.* RONA *is holding a desk diary and a pen.*

RONA. So what do you think about an interview with *The Harvard Crimson*?

CECILIA. The *Crimson*? Oh no. No. Haven't I got another tutorial right now? No.

CECILIA *picks up a tin from her desk and takes a handful of pills with water.*

RONA. The directions state that the maximum is two pills a day.

CECILIA. Fuck the directions. 'Get some good publicity'! Fred said. A student publication will not change the faculty's bias, Rona. I need the *New York Post* – I need the prestige of *The Boston Globe*, *The London Times* –

RONA. Well, a student publication is what you've got! And everyone at Harvard and in Cambridge reads it. What harm can it do?

CECILIA. Harm! Huh! Look at my diary. Do I have time?

She suddenly realises that the ash will go over the pages if she doesn't find her ashtray – which is somewhere. She gets up and bangs her knees on the desk. This knocks the ash off and her coffee over—a mess.

Sonofabitch. Pass me that roll.

RONA *rushes over to help move pages before the coffee spreads.*

RONA. That isn't very nice.

SALLY *pops her head around the door.*

CECILIA. I'm only nice in public, Rona.

SALLY. Hello? Miss Stewart? Professor Gaposchkin?

CECILIA. Don't move a thing. I know exactly where everything is. Pass me that roll of paper?

RONA. Where?

CECILIA. Under the books! It's there for precisely this reason.

SALLY. Miss Stewart?

SALLY *finds the roll and passes it to* RONA.

RONA. What? Oh. Thank you.

CECILIA. What wouldn't I give for a day – one day –

To get up from this desk without banging my knees.

CECILIA *holds up some dripping papers. Looking up at* SALLY.

SALLY. I'm Sally Kane – a staff writer at the *Crimson*.

(*To* RONA.) Is it possible to have a word with Professor Gaposchkin now?

CECILIA. No.

RONA *takes the bundle of pages.*

RONA. Yes.

CECILIA. Are they my students' PhD drafts?

RONA. I'll dry them.

RONA *cleans up.*

SALLY. Is this a bad time?

RONA (*dry*). It's always a bad time. (*Whispering to* SALLY.) You've got five minutes, kid.

CECILIA. Come in. Welcome. When Rona mentioned a *Harvard Crimson* interview I expected one of those floppy-haired young men.

SALLY. Thank you. Yes, there are a few of us girls now.

CECILIA. I used to edit the observatory publication, albeit secretly, for Harlow Shapley.

RONA. Albeit secretly as Harlow Shapley.

CECILIA. I loved the hurly-burly of the Harvard printing office.

SALLY. It's an attractive world, I agree. I must congratulate you on your life's work. You're an inspiration to young women.

CECILIA. My tenured professorship is not so much a personal honour but an indication of our advance in all academic fields. However, it has only taken thirty years to get here.

SALLY. Thirty years?

CECILIA. It passed by in a flash. What are you studying?

SALLY. History.

RONA (*looking up from separating wet PhD pages*). Don't get distracted writing for the *Crimson*.

SALLY. In truth, I'm ready for exams. I'm repeating my final year.

CECILIA. Repeating the year?

SALLY. I had to take time off because of illness.

CECILIA. What rotten luck.

SALLY. It's fine. I'm cramming and doing a stenography course on campus. I dream of a life in writing.

CECILIA. A career in publishing, perhaps?

SALLY. I fear the opportunities are mainly secretarial.

CECILIA. One has to push forward regardless.

SALLY. Exactly. Hence – the profile.

CECILIA. So, this profile… Tell me more.

SALLY. Yes – it's a monthly column detailing the achievements of outstanding faculty members.

RONA. That's what I told you, Mrs G.

SALLY. This is quite the opportunity for me. These articles often get picked up by the nationals in search of material.

RONA (*gently nudging* CECILIA). They do? Hmm…

CECILIA (*picking up* The Boston Globe). Rona, I appear to have Prime Minister Eden's face tattooed on my desk.

RONA *takes the paper from* CECILIA *and bundles it up.*

SALLY. At least it isn't Khrushchev.

CECILIA. Yes, he's made rather a splash in *The Boston Globe*.

SALLY. He's threatened us with nuclear annihilation!

CECILIA. I don't believe the Russians have the capability to launch an intercontinental ballistic missile. What do you think?

SALLY. I, I, I'm sure I don't know.

SALLY *self-consciously takes out her pen and notebook and sets them down as* CECILIA *reorganises her desk.*

CECILIA. Well. It's not like I have him on direct line. I simply think Mr Khrushchev and Co. talk a good game.

RONA *pushes the newspaper into a waste-paper basket.*

SALLY. Your husband – Sergei Gaposchkin –

RONA *looks up sharply at* SALLY.

CECILIA. Oh God, we're not going to talk about him, are we?

SALLY (*spotting* RONA *shaking her head*). Oh sure. No. May I mention in the profile that your husband also works at the Harvard Observatory?

CECILIA *puts her feet up on the table.*

RONA. Sergei and Professor Gaposchkin are writing a book together entitled – *The Galactic Novae.*

CECILIA. It's a systematic analysis of old stars who suddenly with a burst of new energy wow the heavens with pyrotechnics before buggering off to live in quiescence.

RONA *winces at 'buggering off'.*

SALLY. Okay. Um. That's a book I'd read.

SALLY *turns a page of Norman's notebook.*

CECILIA. That's a long list of questions. Let me see and I'll fly through them.

SALLY. My colleague gave me the list –

She puts the notebook back into her bag.

He doesn't know much about science.

CECILIA. Plough your own furrow.

RONA. That's right.

SALLY. Yes! So in the Harvard catalogue, I read that after your BA in Physics and Chemistry at Cambridge, you came all by yourself to study Astronomy at Harvard in 1923.

CECILIA. I had to. Women were not awarded degrees at Cambridge until 1948 – despite doing the same coursework as the men. The only way to pursue postgraduate studies was to come to America.

SALLY. But why astronomy?

CECILIA. I knew I wanted to give my life to astronomy in my first year at Cambridge. I attended a lecture by Arthur Eddington. He detailed how he confirmed Einstein's Theory of Relativity with his 1919 total solar eclipse expedition to the Island of Príncipe.

RONA. This 'confirmation' made Einstein world-famous.

CECILIA. Yes, thank you, Rona, and it made Eddington a household name. You need to understand that it transformed the landscape.

After the lecture, I was on fire – and the cusp of a nervous breakdown.

RONA. Don't put down 'nervous breakdown'.

(*Looking over* SALLY*'s shoulder.*) Just say her career began with a total solar eclipse.

SALLY (*hiding her notes*). I've never seen one.

CECILIA. Ah! The next total solar eclipse that can be seen in Massachusetts…

RONA *jumps up to flick pages of a book on Cecilia's desk.*

RONA. – is in 1959 – October second.

CECILIA. You should join us here at the observatory to witness it.

SALLY. Uhh – I'd like that very much. But back to you. You say you wanted to give your life to astronomy but how difficult was that in the 1920s?

CECILIA (*picking up the telephone from her desk*). If I were to show this telephone to a caveman, he would not be able to comprehend what it is. He'd think it was a nice rock. In the twenties, I was seen as a sort of rock. An annoying rock.

RONA. Progress is slow. She's still a rock.

SALLY. And a rebel? Professor Gaposchkin? Are you one?

CECILIA. Well, I fought against being treated as an inferior, as was sometimes the case in England so yes – probably.

SALLY. And how did our Cambridge compare?

CECILIA. Cambridge, Massachusetts, was intoxicating. The atmosphere was enlightened. I had greater freedom to study what I wished and men did not stamp their feet when I entered a lecture hall!

Let's not be over-enthusiastic about America's freedoms and equalities. There were issues which persist to this day: the exclusion of women and minorities in the sciences.

RONA *clears her throat*. CECILIA *looks at her.*

This is probably not a suitable angle for the *Crimson*.

RONA (*under her breath to* CECILIA). No, it probably isn't!

SALLY. Can you elaborate on the issues that persist today –

RONA. Tell Professor Gaposchkin about your interest in astronomy.

SALLY. Oh, me? Uhh… I was talked out of the sciences at an early age. My mother thinks that women cannot comprehend complex scientific concepts.

CECILIA. Rubbish! Your mother is wrong. Fight for your right to realise the whole of your potential.

SALLY. That's too general a slogan for me.

RONA. Tsshh.

CECILIA. Your horizons are broader than most.

SALLY. You say that but if it's taken you thirty years to achieve what your male peers achieve in five then what hope is there for the rest of us?

CECILIA. Touché. Now tell me, Miss Kane, are you a rebel?

SALLY. You get thrown out of Radcliffe for rebellion.

CECILIA. I recognise the seeds of an outlier though.

SALLY. You do?

There is a moment between them – attraction. RONA *taps her watch to show* CECILIA.

RONA. Mr Questel!

CECILIA. My five o'clock. Can we ask him to wait?

RONA. He's catching a train.

RONA *gestures to* SALLY *to go.*

SALLY. This column goes to print on Thursday. The turnaround is pretty quick. I could write a general overview of your career, of course, but face-to-face would be preferable.

RONA. Yes, yes. Pushy, pushy. I remember.

CECILIA (*checking her diary*). I'm free just after five tomorrow.

SALLY. I'll be here.

CECILIA. Thank you so much, Miss Kane. I'm thrilled the *Crimson* is interested.

RONA *ushers* SALLY *out and hands her some books.*

RONA. A little light reading for you.

SALLY. Thank you for your kindness.

SALLY *exits.*

CECILIA. You can tell Mr Questel to come in.

RONA. Well? Might this student publication you dismissed be useful?

CECILIA. Rona – you're always right. I often find that a tedious quality, but today, I rather appreciate it.

RONA. Praise. At last.

RONA *exits.*

Scene Seven

The Harvard Crimson *newspaper office. Some hours later, after Sally's meeting with CPG.* SALLY *is with* NORMAN, *flicking through the books* RONA *gave her.*

The office looks like a dormitory room in the middle of exams, with rejected term-paper rough drafts covering the floor.

NORMAN *is reviewing Sally's notes.*

NORMAN. Is this it? Didn't you ask about her political beliefs?

SALLY. Take it easy. It was just a preliminary conversation. I've secured the interview for tomorrow And I hope to God it's without her gatekeeper assistant.

NORMAN. Okay. So what's Gaposchkin like?

SALLY. Very English. Impressive. I was pretty nervous but I felt she warmed to me.

NORMAN. It's good if Gaposchkin bonds with you. She'll tell you more. That's why I suggested you. You're very likeable.

SALLY. During my time at Radcliffe I've learnt that men fight the wars, write the books, create the art, and write the symphonies. But she is one of those men.

(*Holding up Rona's books.*) I mean – the scholarship!

NORMAN. Don't get star-struck. You need to be focused.

Did she say anything intriguing during your however brief conversation?

SALLY. She made a comment about Khruschev.

NORMAN. What comment?

SALLY. But she sounds like my father when he gets going on Russia. She said Khrushchev talks a good game.

NORMAN. What else did she say?

SALLY. Come to think of it, perhaps the conversation was more politicised than I realised. She spoke of women and minorities! She bemoaned their exclusion in the sciences.

NORMAN. Did she criticise the government?

SALLY. No. Perhaps she would have if her assistant had left us.

NORMAN. Did you see any political literature lying around?

SALLY. Her office is a bomb site. If you wanted to find anything you'd have to search through papers and cigarette ash.

NORMAN. Maybe I'll do that.

SALLY. Seriously? What exactly are you looking for?

NORMAN. Evidence of her fitness or otherwise to become Chairman at Harvard. However, a clue is in the job title.

SALLY. Surely that's for Harvard to decide.

NORMAN. You'd think – but President Pusey is openly an anti-anti-communist.

SALLY. A lot of professors are.

NORMAN. And pretty much the whole damn lot are in and out of HUAC hearings all the time. It's not just me but many students are alienated by Harvard's leftward drift.

SALLY. They're not writing for *The Harvard Crimson*, are they?! The editorial board is big on free speech, academic freedom and all that.

NORMAN. That's why *we've* got to do something. Now, I told you how communists reveal themselves.

SALLY. Any favourable mention of communism is Un-American. I know.

NORMAN. Yeah but note any talk about 'McCarthyism', 'violation of civil rights', 'racial or religious discrimination'. You'll probably need to steer the conversation – but then you'll get the quotes, right?

SALLY. It's one thing to be provocative in a student newspaper, and I'm happy to do that, but if you're suggesting I guide her, in bad faith, to say something incendiary…? That is a different ball game.

NORMAN. And you want to be a journalist?! Don't stumble at the first hurdle.

NORMAN *hands her an envelope.*

For your trouble.

She looks inside.

SALLY. Fifty dollars! Who's this from?

NORMAN. Let's just say – it's not from *The Harvard Crimson*. Are you against money?

SALLY. Not in principle but I don't want it.

NORMAN. Take it. I know you like to be independent.

SALLY. I'm not going to lie about what Professor Gaposchkin says.

NORMAN. I don't want you to lie. I want you to get to the truth. The woman has been openly critical of the loyalty oath and McCarthy. That's a matter of public record. There's a file on her too.

SALLY. How do you know?

NORMAN. There are investigators at work in every university. Continuous but quiet watchfulness. Do you get me?

SALLY. Are you talking about the FBI?

NORMAN. I know a guy… Another veteran.

SALLY. Isn't spying illegal?

NORMAN. Watchfulness is not illegal. I volunteered out of patriotism. Sally, the communist threat is among us – working the system – influencing the minds of students – our future leaders.

Poland, Hungary, Bulgaria, Romania, Czechoslovakia, Albania, East Germany. Do you think the Soviets are going to stop there? Why should they?

SALLY. I'm a history major. I'm well aware the aggressor never stops himself – he has to be stopped. But can we just get things in perspective here? This is someone's livelihood we're talking about.

NORMAN. I had good buddies in my outfit who died defying communism. I'm just asking you to smoke her out. That's it.

SALLY. I know, I know.

NORMAN. And you've connected with Gaposchkin – you've done the research. You have to do it now. Don't you want your first journalism credit?

SALLY. I want to do the right thing.

NORMAN. Then just do it. Do the right thing. Okay? I need something juicy before the Harvard Corporation makes its decision.

SALLY. No, I'm sorry. I'm crazy about you, but – this is not who I am.

NORMAN. Oh, I know who you are. I know the names of your parents, I know that Harvard man Robert Wise took your virginity in 1955, and your mother is passing off your daughter as her niece's child.

SALLY. I told you that in strict confidence. You swore never to mention it.

NORMAN. You wanted in so badly. I came through for you. Do you think it's going to be this easy when you leave Radcliffe?

SALLY (*wary*). Do you even care for me?

NORMAN. Of course I care. I went to some trouble to get you on the *Crimson*. Do you think they even wanted a girl? I mean – do you care?

SALLY. I do.

NORMAN. You and me? We look like all the kids around here but we're different. We've lived. Right? It's why we click.

Beat.

SALLY. I'll get half an hour with her – tops – and you've got all these questions about her activities during the war. Like – how would I know that? I'm just a student.

NORMAN. You're always going on about how smart you are. You'll figure it out. And that stuff about you? You don't want anyone finding out…

SALLY. I don't.

NORMAN. Good. I'm so glad. So *do* the right thing.

Applause into –

Scene Eight

July 1929. A press conference. Day.

The flash of press cameras. RUSSELL *is spotlit behind a desk holding up a science journal. Applause.*

RUSSELL. Thank you. I will now take questions.

BUDD PHILIPS. Sir? Budd Philips here, science reporter for *The New York Times –*

RUSSELL *puts the journal down.*

RUSSELL. Yes, Mr Philips.

BUDD PHILIPS. Firstly, I'm impressed by your paper: 'On the Composition of the Sun's Atmosphere'. I ate it up.

RUSSELL. Thank you. I hope you digested it well?

BUDD PHILIPS. Indeed! I find it fascinating that you and Eddington staked your reputations on the uniformity of nature theory and now you appear to have changed your mind completely.

RUSSELL (*evades*). For years, Mr Philips, many of us have been puzzling over the question of hydrogen. It was in the air, so to speak.

BUDD PHILIPS. Has there been a race? To find the answer?

RUSSELL (*stalls*). A race? I tussled with the answer for some time but needed to develop a theoretical formula.

BUDD PHILIPS. It must have been quite something to tell Sir Arthur Eddington his theory on stellar constitution was wrong.

BUDD PHILIPS *is touching on some uncomfortable truths.*

RUSSELL. Eddington's work is, of course, hugely influential.

BUDD PHILIPS. How did Eddington react?

RUSSELL. Look, I had to question my own long-held beliefs and embrace flexibility. I needed iron-clad proof. But I do not believe human beings can ever attain an absolute knowledge of God's Universe.

BUDD PHILIPS. Well, Professor Russell, you stand with Copernicus, Newton and Einstein in bringing us a new view of the universe.

RUSSELL. No, really – that's too much. There is still work to be done.

BUDD PHILIPS. Yes, sir, it has taken a brave man to challenge Eddington. And that you are!

Camera flashes.

Scene Nine

1956. Cecilia's office.

Evening. CECILIA *is sitting at her office window. She is writing at a small desk. The moon is visible.*

It's a starry night. The room is lit only by a small desk lamp. RONA *enters.*

RONA. Don't you want more light?

CECILIA *looks up from her work.*

CECILIA. Hmm? I need to send the publisher an index of novae which should come after the main index.

RONA *tidies up around* CECILIA. *Moving teacups –*

RONA (*muttering and mothering*). In the dark like this! Bad for your eyesight.

CECILIA (*gesturing to pages*). Can you double-check the dates of the novae? I've done it from memory.

RONA. That's a tomorrow job, Mrs G. It's night-time! You know, dinner and sleep? All those nice things human beings do.

RONA *empties ashtrays –*

CECILIA (*gesturing to the night sky*). Ursa Major is in fine fettle. My father died over fifty years ago, and I can still see him holding the little me to the night sky – whispering:

(*With her finger tracing from the panhandle of Ursa Major to the top of the rim.*) 'Alkaid, Mizar, Alioth, Megrez, Phecda, Merak, Dubhe'… Then he died – twenty-sixth of December, 1904. Christmases after that were sad affairs…

RONA. I guess you heard that Henry Norris Russell is poorly.

CECILIA (*nods*). It's hard to imagine – all that energy and power – disappearing.

RONA. I thought you didn't like him?

CECILIA *goes back to her writing.*

CECILIA. I don't. But send Mrs Russell some flowers on my behalf.

RONA. Anything else?

CECILIA. I'm going to keep working tonight, Rona. You go on.

RONA *heads for the door but then stops.*

RONA. Mrs G, I've been thinking – does it matter so much if you don't make Chairman? It's a hell of a job. You will have no time for writing and research. And you have been garlanded with so many accolades throughout your lifetime. Isn't that enough?

CECILIA (*sharply*). Enough? Don't be ridiculous. Would Edmund Hillary have been happy going halfway up Everest and saying – 'You know what, Tenzing? It's a bit cold, I think this is far enough!'

RONA (*sharply*). Forget it! Forget I spoke!

CECILIA. It's just that the chairmanship matters, Rona. I don't seek it because I relish departmental bureaucracy nor do I wish to manage colleagues and hear their bloody tedious complaints – it's simply that I will do a better job of chair than anyone else. It's logical. If I had gone into medicine I would have wanted to be a head surgeon, not a nurse. If I had a religious fervour I wouldn't be looking at becoming a nun – I'd –

RONA. You'd want to be Pope.

CECILIA. I'd settle for Cardinal. But I can't be sidelined again.

RONA. Okay. I understand. Well, let's pray the faculty are behind you.

CECILIA. As a child, I conducted an experiment to examine the efficacy of prayer. I divided my school exams into two groups and prayed for one group and not the other. I succeeded in the exams I did not pray for. The thing is, Rona, no matter how talented we are or how hard we work, we are subject to the vagaries of chance. Only fools believe that they are in any control of their destiny.

RONA. So true. So wise. Would you like me to sit with you while you ponder fools and destiny?

CECILIA. No. Go meet Bruce – or whatever your silly young man is called.

RONA. Bruce and I broke up. I didn't want to mention it, but I am pretty upset really.

CECILIA. Well, consider the research you have conducted on stellar evolution. No man will ever give you such a thrill. And now you can concentrate fully on your work without worrying if Bruce will call. Undoubtedly you will be happier. Now, that is something to think about.

RONA. I have thought about it and wholly and respectfully reject your advice. Astronomy is not a cure for heartbreak.

CECILIA. Love is merely a madness, and, I tell you, deserves as well a dark house and a whip as madmen do –

RONA. That Shakespeare fellow knew what he was talking about! Do you need anything before I go?

CECILIA. No, no. Well, don't let me keep you. Goodnight, and forget Bruce, he's a horse's ass. Please remember you are Miss Stewart, summa cum laude from Bryn Mawr, a brain the size of Canada – violinist extraordinaire, a girl I adore.

RONA. Goodnight, Mrs G. Appreciate that.

RONA *exits.* CECILIA *sighs – now free to be melancholic, she turns off the light and sits in the room 'lit' by the moon. After a few moments, someone enters the room and heads to Cecilia's desk.*

CECILIA *watches as the figure moves through the room. A torchlight scans the desk.*

CECILIA. Hello? Who's there? The light is by the door.

The person drops the torch.

What are you doing?

CECILIA *flicks on her desk lamp and sees a man* (NORMAN) *exiting sharpish.*

Who are you? What do you want?

But he's gone.

Scene Ten

Cecilia's office.

The following day. 5 p.m. SALLY, *stylish and demure, with a ribbon in her hair – is looking at* CECILIA, *who is surveying a blurry photograph/glass plate with affection.*

CECILIA. This is Cassiopeia A; which is a remnant of a giant star that went supernova some time in the 1600s. Death becomes her. You'll need to come closer.

SALLY. I'm afraid I know nothing about supernovae.

CECILIA. But supernovae are so exciting. Stars, like humans, die, but theirs is a glorious violent fiery death. They never cease to surprise with their unpredictable timing and sudden outbursts.

CECILIA *carefully puts the glass plate somewhere in the mess of her office.* SALLY *strives to offer something in return.*

SALLY. I've been very taken with the idea that we all are a little piece of stardust.

CECILIA. Beautiful. To think that our DNA was made in the core of giant stars that burst their guts into space billions of years ago.

SALLY. I try to absorb that idea, but it's baffling.

CECILIA. Yes – we are children of the stars.

CECILIA *notices that* SALLY *appears to be staring at her.*

Anyway, we should probably get on.

SALLY. Thank you so much for allowing me to interview you.

CECILIA. I've been tasked with raising my profile so you may yet be doing me a favour.

SALLY. Uhhh… so from my reading, I gather that you were the first to discover that the stars were principally made of hydrogen and helium when you were writing your PhD thesis? How did you dare say that at age twenty-five?

CECILIA. Once you see something, you can't unsee it. You understand?

SALLY. Oh sure. But you modified your findings on the advice of the esteemed astronomer Henry Norris Russell, director of the Princeton Observatory – your external adviser?

CECILIA. He was my assessor, too. That is correct.

SALLY. But Henry Norris Russell portrayed this discovery as his own in 1929.

CECILIA. Why do you say that?

SALLY. I had a seminar with Rona before I arrived.

CECILIA. Ahh, Rona, the keeper of the flame. Let's say Russell was credited with the discovery.

SALLY. So, did Professor Russell steal your findings?

CECILIA. No, I wouldn't say so. He mentions me in his paper.

SALLY. It's a very brief mention. A footnote even.

CECILIA. What you need to know about Russell is that his father and grandfather were both Presbyterian ministers. When Russell faced something he couldn't understand he reasoned it was divine mystery. The universe is subject to laws created by God and so on.

SALLY. But you figured it out.

CECILIA. I used new physics to calculate the temperature scale for stars. The methodology was not widely understood.

SALLY. If you had been a male student would Russell have allowed you to present your findings?

CECILIA. Who knows? But like hydrogen, I was seen as the lightest element – an incongruity, and I was soon to be seeking work in a male world – Russell was probably right to discourage me.

SALLY. Oh?

CECILIA. In science, you must be extremely careful if you challenge views that would overturn decades of belief.

SALLY. Even if you are right?

CECILIA. Especially if you are right, you will be attacked by those whose life's work you are challenging.

SALLY. Shouldn't you defend your position if you are sure of your facts?

CECILIA. Sometimes, you must go along to get along.

SALLY. But you didn't go along with the prevailing thinking.

CECILIA. An outsider can sometimes see more clearly but astronomy is a conservative world. Caution is the watchword if you want to survive.

SALLY. Are you in any way angry or bitter? I mean – Russell came to the same conclusions some four years later.

CECILIA *lights another cigarette.*

CECILIA. Well, you have to consider the times.

Beat.

I was edged out of theoretical astrophysics after that into more routine work. That was disappointing.

SALLY. Professor Gaposchkin, I think your discovery is up there with Newton's Laws of Motion and Darwin's Theory of Evolution.

CECILIA. That's very flattering. Nothing compares with being the first person in the history of the world to see something, but timing is everything. The world has to be ready for you.

SALLY (*writing*). Say if the world is never ready for you?

CECILIA. I prefer to believe –

'There is a tide in the affairs of men.
Which, taken at the flood, leads on to fortune'.

SALLY. So… wait for the tide, huh?

CECILIA. Quite. So, what do you want to do with your life, Miss Kane?

SALLY. Don't let's talk about me. I'm here to interview you.

CECILIA. I congratulate you. You're the first young person I've met who has no interest in talking about themselves. But you must be looking forward to returning to your History degree.

SALLY. To be honest, my parents think I'm wasting my time at Radcliffe.

CECILIA. What are you – twenty?

SALLY. Twenty-one. May I have a cigarette?

CECILIA *passes her the pack.* SALLY *takes one, and* CECILIA *leans in to light her cigarette.*

CECILIA. My daughter is nearly twenty. She's at Swarthmore studying Russian – she wanted to understand her father's heritage and get as far away as possible from Cambridge and me. I don't suppose I was a perfect mother. But I had to put my work first. To get what you want – you have to be a bit selfish –

SALLY. The thing is, I don't have a great talent like you have.

CECILIA. You shouldn't say that.

SALLY. I was top of my class at Riverdale Country Day School. At Radcliffe, I am not even close. However, this self-knowledge has left me without an anchor.

CECILIA. I became a Quaker in my twenties. It's a rather beautiful religion… quite stabilising.

SALLY. I'm descended from Puritans but uh – Quakerism is a little too non-conformist for me. No, I don't need the spiritual. I need purpose. You know some girls in my year are already engaged. Soon my life will revert to home and family. And, of course, that is the natural way – so this feels like my time to find a social or political cause…

CECILIA. You're privileged to be at Radcliffe. You choose your path! Find the causes that align with your values and participate. The country needs you! If I were a student now, I suppose I would be quite fired up. There are very inspiring civil rights debates on campus.

SALLY. I've seen that. Yes. I understand that you and your husband used to run vivid political debates at Harvard during the war. What was that like?

CECILIA. They were not exactly political but rather a series of debates on international questions of the day.

SALLY. You make it sound quite decorous, but you gave people with extreme opinions a platform. There were fisticuffs.

CECILIA. We made mistakes. That's true. Sergei and I chaired these debates, and in a misguided attempt at impartiality, it was unclear which side we were on. It came back to haunt us with the ghastly McCarthy business. But this is way before your time.

SALLY. But you must have been politically engaged at that point.

CECILIA. It was the war! Everyone was politically engaged. And, of course, Russia became a crucial ally.

SALLY. I would quite like to see Leningrad, but I can't imagine when it would be possible to visit. Do you have any plans to go – given your husband's connections?

Beat.

CECILIA. It wouldn't be a good idea for Sergei to return home.

SALLY. Why?

CECILIA. He is an American citizen.

SALLY. I guess that would not go down well with the Politburo.

CECILIA. It's now known as the Presidium.

SALLY. Your students must be so curious about your politics – given your Russian surname.

CECILIA. I don't believe I've ever discussed politics with my students.

SALLY. Not even when Oppenheimer was appointed the William James Lecturer here at Harvard? Quite a number of students protested his appointment.

CECILIA. Not even then.

SALLY. What did you think about Harvard's appointment of Oppenheimer?

CECILIA. His lecture series begins next spring. Things may have calmed down by then.

SALLY. I think it is more likely that the number of protesters will rise. And you haven't answered my question.

CECILIA. I don't want to be quoted.

SALLY. Off the record.

CECILIA. The government's loss is Harvard's gain. And even the Atomic Energy Commission's special review board did not find Oppenheimer disloyal.

SALLY. But he was deemed a security risk all the same.

CECILIA. It's a tricky issue.

Beat.

Do you watch television, Miss Kane?

SALLY. Television?

CECILIA. Yes – we are digressing.

SALLY. I'm afraid I love television.

CECILIA. I ask because my children adore a tedious show called *I Love Lucy*, and everyone I meet seems to be watching it.

SALLY. Tedious? How so?

CECILIA. In every episode, Lucy returns to domesticity after a failed attempt at independence. She's too stupid to do anything without the help of her husband.

SALLY. It's just entertainment. And in real life – Miss Ball is a star who helped her Cuban husband.

CECILIA. So, she has to hide her power to make America love her?

SALLY. You said that sometimes you must 'go along to get along'.

CECILIA. Perhaps I'm being unfair. But I bring it up because she and her husband had a torrid time recently.

SALLY. Lucille Ball admitted to being a signed-up communist.

CECILIA. Miss Ball was cleared of all charges, was she not? She signed up to please a grandparent.

SALLY. But why would Miss Ball sign up for communism if she didn't mean it?

CECILIA. People do many things they don't fully understand, Miss Kane.

SALLY. It seems to me you are just excusing irresponsible decisions unless you mean people like Miss Ball are dumb.

CECILIA. Do you understand the historical and social reasons why people got mixed up in the Communist Party? To fight fascism. To advocate for workers' rights. These are not bad objectives!

SALLY. It's hard to reconcile that with the murderous absolutism of communism.

CECILIA. I think it's still fair to say that some people were driven by idealism and were not in command of the facts. As we have discussed, my husband is Russian –

SALLY. Yes, yes.

CECILIA. He collected blankets for the Russian war relief, he unwittingly signed up to American Soviet organisations and it caused us a deal of trouble.

SALLY. How so?

CECILIA. We were thought to be dangerous radicals. You alluded to this earlier when you mentioned political meetings during the war.

SALLY. I didn't mean to suggest –

CECILIA. It was an unpleasant time.

SALLY. Do you think it affected your academic advancement?

CECILIA (*dismissively*). I doubt it.

SALLY. You must have been pretty angry at America because of these difficulties.

CECILIA. I am grateful to America. She gave me the opportunity to follow the profession that I so desired. My children are American.

SALLY. Yes, of course, they –

CECILIA. There's something about you that doesn't add up.

SALLY. I beg your pardon?

CECILIA. This childish ribbon in your hair. The sweet costume – doesn't match your astute line of questioning.

Beat.

SALLY. I'm honestly lost for words.

CECILIA. Why?

SALLY. I… feel I have offended you in some way.

CECILIA. Put your pen down.

SALLY. My pen?

CECILIA. Can I see your notes?

SALLY. They are in shorthand…

CECILIA. Are you refusing to show me?

Beat.

SALLY. No. Not at all. Here.

SALLY *passes the pages to* CECILIA. CECILIA *flicks through them.* SALLY *holds her breath in fear. After a moment –*

CECILIA. You're right. I haven't the foggiest idea what you've written.

SALLY. I can read it to you.

CECILIA. That won't be necessary. This is off the record. Well – it's like this, Sally, over the years, we've had informants visit the observatory in various guises as assistants or students. Their mission is to catch a 'Red'. The language of anti-communism is not known for nuance, so you recognise when the conversation becomes an interrogation. Their names are often John or David, and invariably, they feed back to the FBI – as evidenced when one or other of us gets a tap on the shoulder. Perhaps it's a step forward if they employ female informants – quite an audacious move to use the disguise of a student paper interview.

SALLY *is taken aback but stands her ground.*

SALLY. I'm simply writing one thousand words on your Harvard career. I intend to be thorough. You can call the office if that is a help?

CECILIA. Then why are you asking me about events that happened a decade ago? Are you angling for an exposé?

SALLY. Oh, my. No. That's not the *Crimson* brief. You and your husband are… kind of legendary. I was being nosy if anything…

CECILIA *stalks around for a moment or so.* SALLY *stays very still – unsure of what she should do next. After a moment…*

Professor Gaposchkin? I'm sorry. You see – I've never interviewed anyone before. I'm probably very clumsy. Do you wish to continue?

Beat.

CECILIA. I've been incautious. That's a liability in astronomy.

SALLY. I'd like to keep going.

CECILIA. Okay.

CECILIA *reaches under her desk and pulls out a bottle of vodka. She grabs tumblers off the desk, dumping pens and elastic bands from them. After wiping them, she pours in vodka. She fills a spare glass with water from a nearby jug and places it beside* SALLY.

It's Polish vodka with gold leaf. I made a disturbing discovery when I accidentally tipped a glass of it into my kitchen sink, and it bleached the tea stains away. Cheers! Nah-zda-*rovh*-yeh!

CECILIA *holds up her glass.* SALLY *ignores her drink.* CECILIA *hands her the glass.*

Now you.

SALLY. Ah. (*She sips a little and winces.*) Bracing.

CECILIA *pushes the glass of water towards* SALLY.

CECILIA. I should apologise. I'm sorry to accuse you like that. I've been feeling embattled for various reasons, but that's no excuse.

SALLY. Please, there's no need.

CECILIA. Your first interview. Here's to firsts. And to answer your earlier question – I am angry and bitter. It's unnecessary to point out what is obvious.

SALLY. I didn't intend to be rude.

CECILIA. You intended to provoke. So here it is. My rage is a caged animal. I cannot be open about disappointment. There's no place for it. Since 1925, I have been upset at Henry Norris Russell's rejection of my hydrogen conclusions. A long time to bear a grudge. It would have made a world of difference – to my life, but it's my fault. I should have had the courage of my convictions! Christ, it's shit being a woman sometimes. Is the *Crimson* ready for that?

SALLY. I'm not sure anyone is, Professor Gaposchkin.

CECILIA. Well – paranoid professor pissed on Polish vodka. There's your profile headline.

(*Drinks.*) 'The mind is its own place and in itself can make a heaven hell, a hell of heaven.' *Paradise Lost.*

CECILIA *peers at* SALLY *who meets her eye.*

SALLY. '*Paradise Lost* is a book once put down, it is very hard to pick up again.' Doctor Samuel Johnson.

CECILIA. Ha! Look, I don't know if I've said anything interesting or helpful for this interview, but it would be best if you didn't say anything negative about Russell. He's very ill and not expected to improve.

SALLY. I understand.

CECILIA. I've never been very good at publicity or, for that matter, being what I'm not, i.e., submissive or charmingly feminine, but don't stitch me up.

SALLY. Of course not.

Beat.

And to be clear – I've been angry about being treated as a pretty little thing since I was about seven. So there.

SALLY *mistakes the tumbler of vodka for water and knocks it back. She splutters.*

Goddammit! Pardon me! I thought that was water.

CECILIA. I'm glad I'm not the only clumsy person around here. And never fucking apologise for swearing.

SALLY. Sorry. Fuck fuck.

CECILIA. I learnt to swear at Cambridge from all the boys who came back from the Great War. Gosh, I learnt some pretty rum phrases that would make a sailor blush.

SALLY. May I have my notes?

CECILIA *pours* SALLY *a glass of water.*

And another vodka for herself. She hands SALLY *back the notes.*

CECILIA. Miss Kane, where did we get to?

SALLY *checks through various sheets of paper and then finds her notes.*

RONA *enters.*

SALLY. Uh… 'Christ, it's shit being a woman'?

CECILIA. Yes… well… My life in astronomy has been a tale of bloody-minded persistence.

CECILIA *spots* RONA.

Rona! Why are you skulking in the corner?

RONA. I was figuring out an appropriate response to a few things.

CECILIA. Close the door and find a glass.

SALLY (*standing up*). You know, I should probably write this up.

CECILIA. There's no rush, surely? Rona is going to give us the next instalment of her relationship with Bruce. A saga of immense proportions. Like an epic by Walter Scott.

RONA. Miss Kane, you still have some time –

SALLY. No really – I have what I need.

CECILIA. Well – it was nice to talk to you. Don't forget the total eclipse in Massachusetts.

SALLY. The eclipse? Yes. Yes.

SALLY *is out the door.*

RONA. Was it something I said?

CECILIA. Maybe it was something I said.

RONA. As long as you didn't talk politics or swear it will be fine… Hmmm.

CECILIA. Hmmm. She asked me some very odd questions. I wonder if she'll even write an article after all.

RONA. Oh, I'm sure she will. She's young – a bit naive I'd say. But I wanted to let you know that I have it on good authority – the dinosaurs have booked the meeting room on Monday.

CECILIA. Do you happen to know who will be in attendance?

RONA. Professor Cabot.

CECILIA. He's a bastard.

RONA. Dr Schwenger.

CECILIA. I like him.

RONA. Richardson.

CECILIA. Beige. He could go either way.

RONA. Varney?

CECILIA. Not very bright.

RONA. That's all I have. Do you want me to eavesdrop? Hmm? Hmm?

CECILIA. No.

RONA *looks mischievous.*

NO.

Scene Eleven

A noisy bar.

SALLY *is by herself, sipping an old fashioned. Her clothing is markedly less girlish – and she is not wearing a ribbon in her hair.* NORMAN *arrives –*

NORMAN. I've been calling.

He kisses her. The attraction between them still lingers.

SALLY. I got your messages. You must have got mine or you wouldn't be here.

NORMAN. Do you want another?

SALLY. I'm good.

NORMAN (*picking up her glass and smelling the contents*). Huh – hard liquor? What are you trying to prove?

SALLY. Nothing. I like the taste.

NORMAN. Slippery slope. So, where've you been?

SALLY. Rhode Island.

NORMAN. Are your folks still giving golden girl a hard time?

SALLY. It was a good visit.

NORMAN. And the baby? What's her name again? Emily? Amy?

SALLY (*stung*). Emily! Like I said, it was a good visit.

NORMAN. Good, good, good. I'm glad all is good in Rhode Island. Well, you've seen this no doubt?

SALLY. Yes.

NORMAN *places a copy of the* Crimson *on the bar table. He turns to a particular page – he reads.*

NORMAN. 'It's hard to imagine what stars truly are: huge heavenly bodies pouring light and energy into space. British mother of three, Professor Cecilia Payne-Gaposchkin, talks about stars as if they were her friends. Her new book on galactic novae (nova doesn't mean a "new star" but a self-rejuvenating old star who puts on a grand show)' –

Not exactly cutting-edge journalism. Where's the wit? The insight?

SALLY. I wasn't feeling it.

NORMAN. You sure were not.

(*Mimicking* SALLY.) 'Professor Gaposchkin, known as Mrs G to her staff, says: 'Stars are just like human beings – they' –

SALLY. Stop.

NORMAN. Are you trying out for a column in *Good Housekeeping*?

SALLY. Very funny.

NORMAN. And sneaky sneaky to go over my head and deliver to the managing editor. I'd have done a better job of editing at least.

SALLY. True but he appreciated the positive spin on Professor Gaposchkin.

(*Whispers.*) But maybe he's a pinko? Crimson by name Crimson by nature – huh?

NORMAN. Huh! I asked you to do something for me.

SALLY *gives him an envelope.*

SALLY. There's your fifty dollars. I did what you wanted. I asked your questions. Maybe a decade ago the Gaposchkins were incautious with their freewheeling political debates on campus – but look into it and you find they were on the right side of history.

NORMAN. For God's sake, Sally! You weren't tasked with making a judgement call.

SALLY. Oh, but I was. It's just you don't like my judgement. What is it about female advancement that bothers you?

NORMAN. I helped you. Didn't I?

NORMAN *grabs her wrist, albeit discreetly.*

SALLY. Now you're hurting me.

NORMAN *releases her wrist.*

NORMAN. Sorry but God damn it – Why did you do it?

SALLY. You know… it's this damn education. Our professors warn against certainty. We're encouraged to scrutinise orthodoxies and opinions and to arrive at our own conclusions.

NORMAN. So now you're a liberal?

SALLY. No – I believe in law and order, tradition, and free enterprise just like you do, but I don't believe in dirty tactics. We've got to debate openly. And in this cockamamie world, I think it's right that I stick up for what I believe in.

NORMAN. You're living in Cloud Cockamamie Land. The radicals are destroying our best traditions.

SALLY. Does your 'FBI guy' know what's going to happen with Mrs Gaposchkin?

NORMAN. No decision has been made. But I think he's going to drop me. I can't forgive you for that.

NORMAN *looks away. He is not entirely comfortable but he's going to push past any remaining tender feelings.*

You'll be the talk of Radcliffe, Sally. An unmarried mother hiding her past?

SALLY. You'd do that, Norman?

NORMAN. I'm thinking about it.

SALLY. You know, when I first met you – you were broken. You said Korea was a waste, a horror –

NORMAN. I said it was a mess. Basic rule of journalism; get your quotes right.

SALLY. I don't think your buddying up to the Bureau will sit well with our colleagues at *The Crimson*.

NORMAN. You wouldn't dare.

SALLY. You've frightened me, Norman. Happy? I guess a few people will be shocked. Maybe I'll be shunned. I'll have to live with that. But everyone hates a snitch. It gives them the creeps.

NORMAN. Well… We'll just have to see.

NORMAN *leaves.* SALLY *sips her old fashioned.*

Scene Twelve

1956. The Harvard Observatory. An anteroom.

A table. WHIPPLE *is followed by a succession of men (members of the Astronomy Faculty). The* PROFESSORS *enter in their particular way; one is puffing on a cigar, another carries an unruly pile of books, another carries a teacup and saucer, and another has a copy of* The Harvard Crimson. *They speak as they enter and take their seats. When the discussion gets heated they talk over one another –*

CABOT. Will this take long? I'm demonstrating meteoric trajectories of golf balls at noon.

RICHARDSON. And sinking whiskey highballs no doubt, ha, ha.

WHIPPLE. It will take as long as it will take, Frank. Good morning, everybody.

Murmurs of 'good morning' from all.

SCHWENGER. How's life at the Smithsonian? Are we winning the Space Race?

WHIPPLE. The official word is yes, Gerhard.

RICHARDSON. The unofficial word is?

WHIPPLE. It's a state secret, so I could tell you, but then I'd have to kill you. Gentlemen, Miss Anderson is off sick. I will be taking minutes.

CABOT. Double-jobbing, again? Ha, ha.

WHIPPLE. Indeed. Are we all here?

VARNEY. I thought there would be coffee.

CABOT (*relighting his cigar*). So, we are to debate whether to set a precedent.

RICHARDSON. A debate, Professor Whipple? I like a discussion.

WHIPPLE. Shall we begin?

CABOT. Is it the job of our venerable institution to create opportunities for female representation? This is not an ideal approach to identify the best head of department.

WHIPPLE. I happen to believe Professor Gaposchkin is the best man for the job.

RICHARDSON. You say that, but she is temperamental –

VARNEY. And, of course, at her age, women become pretty strange. Sharper, would one say? Or do I mean spikier? Is one allowed to say that of women in middle years?

WHIPPLE. No! And Professor Gaposchkin has reason to be temperamental. The observatory, under Harlow Shapley, hid her away in a cupboard marked 'equipment' for thirty years.

RICHARDSON. She taught me. Excellent, though a little sarcastic.

SCHWENGER (*putting a copy of* The Harvard Crimson *on the table*). Good article about her in Friday's *Crimson*.

RICHARDSON. Yep, seen it.

CABOT *picks up the paper and opens it.*

WHIPPLE. She takes a strong interest in the graduate students. They like and trust her.

SCHWENGER. Undoubtedly, it's a plus. However, think about our current crop of graduate and PhD students. There are two women in an intake of – how many men? Twenty-two?

VARNEY. Good point, Gerhard. Might it deter young men from choosing Harvard?

RICHARDSON. Harvard chooses, James. Not the other way around.

WHIPPLE. A genius is a genius, and so I think we see her as genderless?

CABOT. We? And Gaposchkin's a genius, is she?

RICHARDSON. We all know she wants the job.

VARNEY. Lord knows she's made that abundantly clear.

(*Unwrapping a sandwich.*) Does anyone mind?

CABOT (*reading the* Crimson). Every award the woman has ever won is listed here. Am I the only one to find her ambition distasteful?

SCHWENGER. Oh come off it, Frank, you're always shouting your wares!

CECILIA *enters, unseen by the* PROFESSORS.

RICHARDSON. What about the awful husband? He's always showing off and doing press-ups for the new female graduates and such.

WHIPPLE. We can't get rid of Sergei anyway. He's an employee here.

RICHARDSON. He's so small in comparison with her in every aspect.

Some of the men start to chuckle.

WHIPPLE. I will not tolerate this adolescent direction of travel.

RICHARDSON *holds up in hands in a 'sorry'.*

WHIPPLE. The appointment of Mrs Gaposchkin could make us appear ahead of the tide.

RICHARDSON. Then again the tide may never come in.

CABOT. Listen, don't you want the campus we remember? I'm sick of discussions about politics and civil rights – these self-righteous debates about progressive philosophies.

SCHWENGER *shakes his head in disbelief.*

What? I'm just saying what a lot of people are thinking.

SCHWENGER. Speak for yourself!

WHIPPLE. Let's keep this cordial. Cecilia is the faculty member with the requisite international recognition. You block her appointment, Pusey may suggest we look outside Harvard.

SCHWENGER. That brings its own hazards.

RICHARDSON. But does she have the fiscal acumen and the long-term vision to run and develop the department?

SCHWENGER. That's a fair point.

CABOT. The department needs a truly powerful person. Has Gaposchkin got the mental strength – the requisite iron in her to manage all the personalities? It's a heck of an undertaking. Fred, your eye has been off the ball for months.

WHIPPLE. Guilty. But am I right in thinking that one or two among you may feel challenged by being evaluated by her?

No response, but one or two shift uncomfortably in their seats.

SCHWENGER. As I said, she's very –

CABOT. Arrogant.	SCHWENGER. – Blunt. But fair.

WHIPPLE. Good. Yes. Gentlemen, are there other good reasons why she shouldn't attain the post?

CABOT. She's mad. Ha, ha, ha.	RICHARDSON. And gets madder than mad –

Some laughter.

WHIPPLE. Enough, Frank! This is a serious matter. We're all prone to outbursts and language unbecoming.

CABOT. More seriously – is she an exciting candidate? She may have been the bright young thing of 1925 but what of consequence has she published recently?

SCHWENGER. Oh, she's published monumental data on variable stars, light curves, eclipsing binaries –

CABOT. Old-fashioned astronomy.

RICHARDSON. Her gender has been a tremendous obstacle to her professional progression, but I agree with Frank, only in the sense that her superior intellect has hardly been exercised recently.

VARNEY. Exercised? She's not a horse.

CABOT. Our dear President Lowell swore that the then Miss Payne should never have a position while he was in office!

WHIPPLE. He's been dead a long time, Frank.

SCHWENGER. I cannot say that I approved President Lowell's decisions on who shouldn't be part of this great institution.

VARNEY. Hear, hear.

CABOT. Not this again!

SCHWENGER. Sir, he barred my Jewish father's application. He attempted to establish a direct quota on Jewish students, he segregated Black students, he purged homosexuals from Harvard – this man cannot be the barometer of decency!

CABOT. I keep telling you – Lowell cannot be criticised for upholding the values and traditions of the 1920s.

SCHWENGER. Outmoded Anglo-Saxon traditions! Which endure.	VARNEY. Easy, man!

WHIPPLE. Isn't it time we stopped listening to dead men?

CABOT. We haven't yet mentioned left-wing inclinations. Did anyone see the *Evening Star*? The stuff about HUAC?

WHIPPLE. Does anyone here know Mrs Gaposchkin's attitude to the atomic bomb? Korea? Federal funding to the university? I tell you, none of us do because she has been careful to keep her political opinions to herself.

RICHARDSON. She's more careful now than she was during the war.

SCHWENGER. Aren't we all careful? Fearful even?

VARNEY. Sorry, but that Russian name is a concern.

SCHWENGER. And the corporation has shown little bravery in their handling of civil liberties –

VARNEY. This constant questioning about our commitment to anti-communism, / there's been so much noise –

RICHARDSON. We all know the pressure President Pusey has been under. That will be the main concern for the Harvard Corporation.

SCHWENGER. Will her appointment affect any of our federal funding?

WHIPPLE. We comply with all of the regulations.

RICHARDSON. We must think of our benefactors –

SCHWENGER. We think of nothing else but we certainly don't want to be in the pockets of wealthy donors who may be uncomfortable with our decisions.

VARNEY. Uhh – I think we are in their pockets whether we like it or not. It is about the money.

SCHWENGER (*regretful*). It is about the money.

RICHARDSON. She's not experienced in accessing government funding. Problem!

CABOT. I fully agree with the Harvard Corporation's public statement that a communist is not fit to be a member of the faculty.

WHIPPLE. Frank, I wish you would stop talking in press statements. Professor Gaposchkin is not a communist.

CABOT. She's all for renewing cooperation with international scientists –

WHIPPLE. And many of us wish to challenge the State Department's restrictive foreign policy directives. It does not serve astronomy to be isolationist.

RICHARDSON. It's tricky though, Fred, isn't it? We want a quiet life.

WHIPPLE. Everything is tricky. We have the choice of a continuity candidate or a roll of the dice with a person unknown to us. Gentlemen, may I finally draw your attention to Professor Gaposchkin's retirement.

RICHARDSON. Retire? Of course.

WHIPPLE. She's fifty-six.

CABOT. Fifty-six! She won't want to keep on much past sixty. There is certainly no woman like her. We wouldn't have to go through this again.

WHIPPLE. Gentlemen, if we stand together, we can resist pressure from the corporation. The most important question is – does Gaposchkin merit the spot? I for one think she more than merits it. I am asking for your unanimous support.

CECILIA. Good morning, gentlemen.

The men stand – taken aback – probably wondering what she heard –

CABOT. Professor Gaposchkin, would you mind waiting outside?

CECILIA. Yes, Professor Cabot, I would mind waiting outside.

WHIPPLE. Please come in.

CECILIA. Thank you. Well, I've been eavesdropping, and I give you seven out of ten for effort and three out of ten for perspicacity.

RICHARDSON (*blustering*). It's simply that we didn't expect to see you.

CECILIA. That is evident, Professor Richardson. I recently had a stimulating conversation with a young woman who used a phrase I often use myself: 'If you are sure of your facts, then you should defend your position.' Firstly, of course, I merit the position. You all know that. I deserve it! I'm the most qualified and experienced scientist here. I could say that it's become harder for us to attract top-flight talent now that MIT has overtaken us. And – Harvard might well bring in a young dynamo who will ruthlessly clear out the old. No one will be safe. But the fact of the matter is, gentlemen, I am not the enemy! We're all scientists.

Let us go forward with the open-minded objectivity that befits the spirit of our great observatory. Now get on with it.

If you'll excuse me I have to get back to work.

She moves to exit –

Don't stand. There's really no need.

But the men do stand as CECILIA *exits.*

A shifting of feet – scratching of heads. A murmur of agreement disgruntled or otherwise.

CABOT. Extraordinary!	VARNEY (*quietly*). How much of that did she hear? Huh?

WHIPPLE. No discussion. A show of hands in favour, please.

WHIPPLE *raises his hand. Then* SCHWENGER –

RICHARDSON *looks around and raises his hand. Followed by* VARNEY.

CABOT *knows he is beaten. He makes a noise – maybe it's a grunt – covering a profanity. Reluctantly and slowly he raises his hand.*

Scene Thirteen

2nd October 1959. The Harvard Observatory Hill. The total solar eclipse.

Watching a sped-up solar eclipse – CECILIA, RONA *and* SALLY *(her outfit a nod to the 1960s).*

There is birdsong in the distance – and atmospheric sound.

They stand before a huge bright Sun – a disturbing shadow crosses.

RONA. The birds have stopped singing. And feel that? It's getting cold –

SALLY. It's like the end of the world.

CECILIA. Or the beginning?

The Moon covers the Sun like a black, crisp circle; a black abyss beyond light or time. The Sun's corona can be seen. It's a magical sight. As the Moon passes on, the Sun emerges. CECILIA *is revealed alone.*

Scene Fourteen

17th January 1977. A stage. The American Astronomical Society. The Henry Norris Russell Prize Lecture.

CECILIA *is spotlit. She is addressing posterity as much as she is addressing the audience. The portrait of Henry Norris Russell is visible, as per Scene One.*

CECILIA. 'The reward of the young scientist is the emotional thrill of being the first person in the history of the world to see something or to understand something. Nothing can compare with the ecstasy of the experience. The reward of the older scientist is the sense of having seen a vague sketch grow into a masterly landscape.'

When I began my career in 1925 the study of the novae was but a sketch. We roughed out more of the design and worked tirelessly to add fine detail. Fifty years later none can claim that the masterpiece is the work of a single hand nor indeed claim it is the final picture. Final and definitive are treacherous last words for the scientist! Ovid reminds us there is nothing constant in the universe.

I began by looking backwards and I would like to end by looking forwards. These words are for the young women I see before me and the generations to come. Only become a scientist if nothing else will satisfy. The material returns aren't great. Fame is the reward of the few.

You'll need to stand strong. These names are a testament to the power of perseverance. Some have been my colleagues.

Others I have admired from afar:

Adelaide Ames, Annie Jump Cannon, Antonia Maury, Margaret Burbidge, Vera Rubin, Henrietta Swan Leavitt, Dorrit Hoffleit, Lise Meitner, Katherine Johnson, Joan Feynman, Shirley Ann Jackson, Margaret J. Geller, Nancy Grace Roman, Jocelyn Bell Burnell.

You see, I'd rather not be the first to win this award but the first of many. Don't let anyone shut you up. Make some noise, ladies!

As a classicist, my father was fond of quoting Ptolemy, and I will leave you with his words:

'I know that I am mortal by nature and ephemeral;

but when I trace the windings to and fro of the heavenly bodies

I no longer touch the earth with my feet. I stand in the presence of Zeus himself and take my fill of ambrosia.'

The light fades. The stars pulse…

Source Material

'Henry Norris Russell Prize Lecture of the American Astronomical Society – Fifty Years of Novae' by Cecilia Payne-Gaposchkin

'American Astronomical Society, Meeting, 149th, Jan. 17, 1977', *Astronomical Journal*, vol. 82, September 1977, https://doi.org/10.1086/112105 © AAS. Reproduced with permission

'The Most Brilliant Ph.D Thesis Ever Written in Astronomy', Owen Gingerich

'So You Want to Do Research', December 1943, *Pro Tem* (Harvard digitised collection)

The Dyer's Hand, Cecilia Payne-Gaposchkin, ed. Katherine Haramundanis

An Autobiography and Other Recollections, Cecilia Payne-Gaposchkin, ed. Katherine Haramundanis

Stars in the Making, Cecilia Payne-Gaposchkin

The Glass Universe, Dava Sobel

Portrait of a Binary, The Lives of Cecilia Payne-Gaposchkin and Sergei Gaposchkin, Sylvia L. Boyd

Henry Norris Russell: Dean of American Astronomers, David H. DeVorkin

Interview of Cecilia Payne-Gaposchkin by Owen Gingerich on 1968 March [online] aip.org/history-programs/niels-bohr-library/oral-histories/4620

What Stars Are Made Of: The Life of Cecilia Payne-Gaposchkin, Donovan Moore

The American Institute of Physics (AIP Oral Histories)

The Fires of the Sun, David Bodanis

'The Ladies of Observatory Hill', George Greenstein, *The American Scholar*, February 1993

Beyond Curie: Four Women in Physics and Their Remarkable Discoveries, 1903 to 1963, Scott Calvin

'Cecilia and Sergei: American Astronomers', *Galactic Gazette*, February 2018

'How to Spot a Communist', US Army Pamphlet

Many Are the Crimes: McCarthyism in America, Ellen Schrecker

'Extraordinary Claims Require Extraordinary Evidence: C.H. Payne H. N. Russell and Standards of Evidence in Early Quantitative Spectroscopy', David H. DeVorkin, *Journal of Astronomical History and Heritage*, Vol. 13

Uneasy Careers and Intimate Lives: Women in Science, 1789–1979, Phina G. Abir-Am and Dorinda Outram (eds.)

Advancing Variable Star Astronomy: The Centennial History of the American Association of Variable Star Observers, Michael Saladyga and Thomas R. Williams

Of Stars and Men: Reminiscences of an Astronomer, Zdeněk Kopal